# The Shenanigans
## of
# Slim Pickins

Story and Illustrations by
**Tony Viehmann**

For Sophie & Jack~
Enjoy Slim!
Tony

**Dedicated to Kiera**, who I hope will grow up
to marvel at seagull antics
as much as her grandfather does.

www.depotpublishing.com   12 Depot Street, Kennebunk, ME 04043
© 2012 Tony Viehmann   ISBN 978-0-615-66327-2

# Introduction

Imagine having a seagull suddenly land on your shoulder, flap its wings, and snatch a chicken salad sandwich right out of your hands - just before you were about to take your very first bite. Then, to add insult to injury, the sneaky bird lands just a few feet away and devours the whole thing right in front of your eyes!

This actually happened to me, and ever since, I have been fascinated observing seagulls at Mothers Beach in Kennebunk, Maine. This story is about one such bird we shall name Slim Pickins. Parts of it are true.

**Slim Pickins** was no ordinary bird. He was a scraggly looking young seagull and almost always up to no good.

Slim was easy to recognize from the other gulls. He was noisy, nosy, and the feathers on top of his head stood almost straight up. Every day was a "bad hair" day for Slim.

Slim LIVED TO EAT! He cruised Mothers Beach every day looking for something to fill his tummy... often someone's lunch!

Considering the amount he ate,
it's a wonder Slim wasn't as big as
a blimp! Instead, he was lean and
mean and quick as a wink. Of all the
gulls on the beach, he was the best
at what he did. The pesky little pick-
pocket knew every trick in the book
to get what he wanted – FOOD,
FOOD, FOOD!

Slim arrived at the beach just around lunchtime. Wings spread, he would glide back and forth overhead checking out the location of all the beach bags.

Slim would then swoop down, make a soft landing in back of where the families were gathered, and rudely announce his arrival with that ear-piercing squawk only a seagull can make.

At first, Slim would prowl around for whatever he could find on the sand – a potato chip here, a pretzel there, maybe even a broken cookie. Slim was never satisfied. He was always on the lookout for the "big hit".

Most of the children would guard their sandwiches or quickly hide them deep down inside the family beach bag when they saw the little pest heading their way. Some never saw him coming.

Slim was smart and ever so patient. He would silently sneak up behind a hungry child about to eat lunch and snatch a sandwich in the blink of an eye. The scruffy little thief would then drop it on the sand and peck away until trouble arrived.

Other gulls would scamper over to steal a morsel or two, but Slim would quickly grab whatever he could, and fly to a safer place to enjoy his prize all by himself. Before long, he would be back for more.

If Slim couldn't steal a sandwich, he had another trick up his sleeve. WAIT. He knew that sooner or later a beach bag full of goodies would be left alone when a family went down to the water for a swim.

The crafty bird would then waddle up to the bag and poke his head deep down inside to see what treasures awaited him. Whenever he got caught in the act, children and parents would chase him away, but he always returned.

One sunny afternoon Slim got very lucky. He was
able to wrestle a meatball sub out of a bag and
devour the entire thing in just under a minute! The
wide-eyed children watched his neck bulge as he
hastened to gulp down each meatball. Something
had to be done!

The beach families gathered together that very afternoon and formed the SLIM PICKINS BEACH PATROL. The children and their parents were determined to teach Slim proper manners one way or another.

What could they do? Indeed Slim was an
unwelcome visitor, but they didn't want to hurt
him. After all, it was his beach too!
The next day the children arrived with squirt guns.
At lunchtime Slim flew in right on schedule for his
afternoon feast.

They thought a few squirts would discourage the little rascal as he went snooping around the beach bags, but not this playful pest. He was quick to dodge any squirts coming his way, and didn't seem to mind the few times he got wet. After all, Slim was a seagull!

What would the Beach Patrol do next?

The parents tried covering their bags with beach towels and heavy rocks, but Slim was very determined, and always found a way to get his head inside the bags when no one was looking.

What would the Beach Patrol do next?

Some of the families brought radios to the beach.
Surely an unruly bird like Slim would not stick
around if they played fancy classical music. Slim
outsmarted them all by changing the station to
Hillbilly Country Western with his pesky pointed
beak.

What would the Beach Patrol do next?

They brought large plastic statues of scary looking owls with bulging eyes and sharp claws to guard their bags. Slim was unafraid, and was even seen snuggling close to one of the owls. Perhaps he was trying to make a new friend!

What would the Beach Patrol do next?

If scary owls didn't work, certainly live dogs would scare him away, but not Slim. He would look the dogs straight in the eyes, flap his wings, and nip at their paws with his beak. Once again, Slim had his way.

What would the Beach Patrol do next?

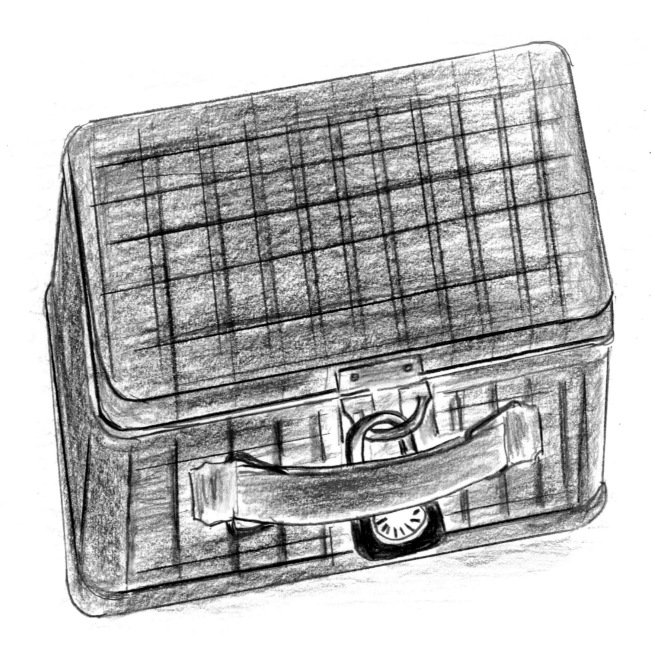

The Beach Patrol met and it was decided that
each family would bring their lunch the next day
in a LOCKED METAL LUNCH BOX. Slim would
finally learn who really ruled the beach.

Wouldn't you know the clever thief soon figured out how to pick the locks, open the lids, and help himself to whatever was inside!

The Slim Pickins Beach Patrol was out of ideas. Even the lifeguards sat in their tower shaking their heads.  They suggested people eat lunch at home but that idea went over like a lead balloon.  No one knew what to do next.

Slim became the "talk of the town." People came from far away to observe the clever little bird in action. Everyone was amazed at Slim's shenanigans.

There was even talk of capturing Slim and taking him on a road trip to show off his tricks, but the Slim Pickens Beach Patrol would not hear of such a foolish idea. Some of the children even called him "cool" and "Houdini" and "Smarty Pants."

One day, everything changed...

Slim arrived at noon, but this time, with a new
friend. She was a proud looking gull with beautiful
white and gray feathers. She was exceedingly well-
mannered as well!

Slim and his lovely friend stayed close together. Whenever he made a move for food, she would wedge herself between Slim and the food, flap her wings, and scold him. The children named her Daisy.

Daisy arrived at the beach every day with Slim at her side. She was quick and nimble when catching small fish in tidepools. Slim did everything she did, and soon learned how to fill his tummy the right way if you are a seagull.

Everyone wondered if Slim had found a gullfriend or, perhaps, Daisy might even be his mother teaching her naughty son how to catch fish for the very first time.

Summer was almost over and the beach families delighted in watching the two gulls hanging out together. Best of all, Slim was minding his manners!

Slim even began to look better. His scruffy feathers disappeared, and he proudly showed off his new white and gray colors as he paraded down the beach looking over at the children eating their lunch.

"What was he thinking?", they wondered.

Daisy knows. Do you?

# About the Author

Tony Viehmann lives on the shore in Cape Porpoise, Maine with his wife Nancy and his golden retriever, Rosa. As a retired teacher and school counselor, Tony continues teaching children about marine life at local school enrichment programs, the Wells National Estuarine Research Reserve, the Kennebunkport Conservation Trust, and at the KBIA summer camp at Mothers Beach. He also enjoys carving whales and dolphins. Tony is a keen observer of whales, dolphins, seals, and shorebirds — especially seagulls! He is often seen rowing his peapod around Stage Harbor with Rosa in the bow.